SELECTED FROM

A DIFFERENT KIND OF CHRISTMAS

ALEX HALEY

WRITERS' VOICES

SIGNAL HILL

WRITERS' VOICES™ was made possible by grants from:
An anonymous foundation; The Vincent Astor Foundation;
Booth Ferris Foundation; Exxon Corporation; James Money
Management, Inc.; Knight Foundation; Philip Morris
Companies Inc.; Scripps Howard Foundation; The House of
Seagram; and the H.W. Wilson Foundation.

• • •

ATTENTION READERS: We would like to hear what
you think about our books. Please send your comments
or suggestions to:

The Editors
New Readers Press
P.O. Box 131
Syracuse, NY 13210-0131

• • •

Selection: From A DIFFERENT KIND OF CHRISTMAS by
Alex Haley. Copyright © 1988 by Kintl Corporation. Used
by permission of Doubleday, a division of Bantam Doubleday Dell Publishing Group, Inc.

SIGNAL HILL

Additional material
© 1991 Signal Hill Publications
A publishing imprint of Laubach Literacy International

10 9 8 7 6 5 4 3 2

ISBN 1-929631-26-9

First printing: March 1991

The words "Writers' Voices" are a trademark of
New Readers Press.

Cover designed by Paul Davis Studio
Interior designed by Helene Berinsky

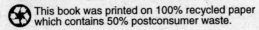

This book was printed on 100% recycled paper
which contains 50% postconsumer waste.

Acknowledgments

We gratefully acknowledge the generous support of the following foundations and corporations that made the publication of WRITERS' VOICES and NEW WRITERS' VOICES possible: An anonymous foundation; The Vincent Astor Foundation; Booth Ferris Foundation; Exxon Corporation; James Money Management, Inc.; Knight Foundation; Philip Morris Companies Inc.; Scripps Howard Foundation; The House of Seagram, and the H.W. Wilson Foundation.

This book could not have been realized without the kind and generous cooperation of the author, Alex Haley, and his publisher, Doubleday, a division of Bantam Doubleday Dell Publishing Group, Inc. Thanks to Carol Christiansen, Permissions Manager.

We deeply appreciate the contributions of the following suppliers: Cam Steel Die Rule Works Inc. (steel cutting die for display); Canadian Pacific Forest Products Ltd. (text stock); ComCom (text typesetting); Horizon Paper Co., Inc. and Domtar Fine Papers (cover stock); MCUSA (display header); Delta Corrugated Container (corrugated display); Phototype Color Graphics (cover color separations); and Arcata Graphics Company/Buffalo (cover and text printing and binding).

Our thanks to Paul Davis Studio and Myrna Davis, Paul Davis, Jeanine Esposito, Alex Ginns and Frank Begrowicz for their inspired design of the covers of these books. Thanks also to Helene Berinsky for her sensitive design of the interior of this book, Karen Bernath for design of maps and diagrams, and Ron Bel Bruno for his timely help.

CONTENTS

NOTE TO THE READER

A Different Kind of Christmas is an adventure story that takes place during the time of slavery in the United States. It is based on historical facts.

The author, Alex Haley, is the man who wrote the book *Roots.* In *Roots,* he told about slavery: how Africans were captured and brought to North America and their experience here as slaves. In *A Different Kind of Christmas,* Haley tells about black and white men and women who opposed slavery and how these people organized to help slaves escape.

Every writer has a special voice. That is why we call our series *Writers' Voices.* We chose *A Different Kind of Christmas* because Alex Haley's voice can be clearly heard. In his books, Alex Haley combines facts from history with his own vision of what happened. In reading this book you will not only discover what happens to the characters, you can also see how Haley puts fact and fiction together. In choosing parts from the book, we wanted you to discover how and why the main character decides to help some slaves escape and to give you the adventure story of the escape itself.

Reading "About the Selections from *A Different Kind of Christmas*" on page 11 will help you begin thinking about what you will read in the selections.

In addition to selections from *A Different Kind of Christmas*, this book includes chapters with interesting and helpful information related to the story. You may read these before or after reading the story. You may choose to read some or all of these chapters.

- If you would like more information about how people—black and white, free and slave—organized to help slaves escape from the South, look at the chapter called "About the Underground Railroad" on page 60.

- Many readers enjoy finding out about the person who wrote the story. Sometimes this information will give you more insight into the story. You can find out more about Alex Haley in the chapter on page 56.

If you are a new reader, you may want to have this book read aloud to you, perhaps more than once. Even if you are a more experienced reader, you may enjoy hearing it read aloud before reading it silently to yourself.

We encourage you to read *actively*. Here are some things you can do.

Before Reading

- Read the front and back covers of the book, and look at the cover illustration. Ask yourself what you expect the book to be about.

- Think about why you want to read this book. You may want to learn about slavery and the Underground Railroad. You may have seen the television program *Roots* and be curious about what another story by the same author is like.

- Look at the Contents page. See where

you can find a chronology, maps and other information. Decide what you want to read and in what order.

During Reading

•There may be words that are unfamiliar to you or words used in ways that are new to you. Alex Haley uses many words that come from the time that the story takes place. Keep reading to see if the meaning becomes clear. If it doesn't, go back and reread the difficult part or discuss it with others. Or look up the words in the dictionary.

•Ask yourself questions as you read. For example: How does a person decide for him- or herself the right thing to do?

After Reading

•Think about what you have read. Did you learn something new about this time in history? Did you get new information about slavery or the Underground Railroad? Did reading this selection make you see people from these times in a new way?

- •Talk with others about your thoughts.

- •Try some of the questions and activities in "Questions for the Reader" on page 50. They are meant to help you discover more about what you have read and how it relates to you.

The editors of *Writers' Voices* hope you will write to us. We want to know your thoughts about our books.

ABOUT THE SELECTIONS FROM
A DIFFERENT KIND OF CHRISTMAS

A Different Kind of Christmas is an adventure story based on historical facts. It takes place during the time of slavery, in 1855, just six years before the beginning of the Civil War (1861–1865). The story is about Fletcher Randall, a young white man from a southern plantation family. Fletcher comes to see that slavery is wrong and helps a group of slaves organize an escape. The escape is planned for Christmas Eve.

The owners of the large farms, or plantations, often had between 50 and 100 slaves. On these plantations, the "house servants" looked after the white family and their home. The "field hands" worked the land. The slaves labored from sunrise to sundown. White overseers often watched the field hands as they worked.

Slaves were treated like property. Some slaveholders and overseers treated the slaves with kindness, but many treated them cruelly. When slaves were bought and sold, family members were often permanently separated from one another.

By 1804, all of the northern states had freed their slaves. But in the years before 1861, when the Civil War began, southern slaveholders became more determined than ever to keep their slaves. This is the period when this story takes place.

When the selection from *A Different Kind of Christmas* begins, Fletcher Randall is in college in the North at Princeton, New Jersey. Back home in North Carolina, Fletcher's family lives on a big plantation with more than 100 slaves. Fletcher's father is an important state senator who is fighting to keep slavery legal.

Fletcher feels caught between two worlds. He is taunted by students from the North who are against slavery. Yet he does not get along with his fellow students from the South, who tease him because he is a serious student. Fletcher is befriended by the three Ellis brothers, from the city of Philadelphia, Pennsylvania, which is near Princeton. The Ellises are Quakers (also known as Friends), a peace-loving religious sect that is opposed to slavery.

During a weekend visit to Philadelphia, the Ellises introduce Fletcher to some freed slaves. They take the young Southerner to an antislavery rally.

This experience shocks and angers Fletcher. He feels betrayed by the Ellises. Yet he is drawn to learn more about the history and the morality of slavery. What he learns changes how he feels. After this, his life will never be the same.

When Fletcher goes back to his family's plantation for the Christmas holidays, he has a secret mission—to help 12 slaves escape to freedom on the Underground Railroad. (You'll find more information about this in the chapter on the Underground Railroad on page 60.)

Perhaps the selections will remind you of a time when you changed your mind about something important. Perhaps you will recall a time when you went against your family's wishes.

*   *   *

In some places, Alex Haley tries to give you an idea of how the characters' speech sounds. This happens especially with one of the slaves, Harpin' John. When this happens, a punctuation mark called an apostrophe (') is used to show that one or two letters were left out. For example, the word *because* may be written *'cause* or *doing* may be written *doin'*.

A DIFFERENT KIND OF CHRISTMAS

ALEX HALEY

Fletcher Randall, the son of a southern slave owner, came to the North to go to college. Here he met three Quaker brothers, the Ellises. They are opposed to slavery. They take him to an antislavery rally.

The Antislavery Meeting

The carriage stopped, and Fletcher saw ahead of them a moderate crowd that seemed to average three white people to each black, all of them filtering and shifting about for better standing places before a small, brownish, covered tent.

As they walked closer, for an instant Fletcher closed his eyes. He had just glimpsed, sitting in folding chairs on the

MAPS OF PLACES MENTIONED
IN THE SELECTIONS

Slave States
Free States
Territories

THE STATES WHERE SLAVERY WAS LEGAL IN 1855

Fifteen states allowed slavery in 1855: Delaware, Maryland, Virginia (which included West Virginia), Kentucky, Tennessee, North Carolina, South Carolina, Georgia, Florida, Alabama, Mississippi, Louisiana, Texas, Arkansas and Missouri.

CANADA

ILLINOIS INDIANA OHIO Philadelphia, PENNSYLVANIA Princeton, NEW JERSEY

Mississippi River Ashe County, NORTH CAROLINA

N

CONTINENTAL UNITED STATES IN 1991

tent stage, two white and two black men wearing dark suits, white shirts, and ties.

Rising abruptly, one of the white men began loudly exhorting the crowd: "More will have to be done to help our black brothers and sisters, whom some call *slaves,* escape to freedom!"

Fletcher stood disbelieving the crowd's applause. Next, a black speaker rose and beckoned toward the audience. Within a moment, climbing the steps while glancing warily over both shoulders was an extremely ragged, barefoot, short, powerfully built black man holding a burlap sack behind his neck to cover his shoulders.

"Maceo here escaped. He hid by day and ran following the North Star at night, despite his overseer and slave hunters with guns and bloodhounds. He just reached safety here night before last, and has been sleeping almost every minute since!"

Amidst the crowd's applause the black speaker paused dramatically. "You think Maceo looks all right to you? Well, just take a look at Maceo's back!"

He pulled the burlap sack off the black

man's shoulders, revealing a mess of welts, some partly healed, others still infected. Amid the horrified sounds of the crowd, many of whom were in tears, the speaker yelled, "Now all hold up your hands who would vote to send Maceo back to slavery!"

"No, no, no!" shouted the crowd. "Well then," cried the speaker, "let's dig deep in our pockets to help the three million more slaves in the South who cannot escape—unless we help!"

The crowd was pressing forward, dropping bills and coins into the black speaker's can, when the second white speaker rose, yelling like a country revival preacher.

"Think of our enslaved black brothers and sisters—tired and weary of chopping down forests to clear new acres to farm for their master! Think of dragging and filling twelve-foot-long cotton-picking sacks that get as heavy as rocks! Think of working your hardest and being beaten and lashed to try and make you work yet harder—to keep your cruel masters and their spoiled families fat and rich! Think of those who have now decided they must *escape* all this! They must *escape* the cotton fields and the rice swamps! Black men and women and their children, and those without any family, their families dead from the perils of slavery, often from being beaten, or worked to death! All over the South, and in the border slave states, they are waiting for the signal to escape! They are waiting to see an Underground Railroad conductor nod, or hear him whisper a snatch of the right song, or hear the hoot owl's call, or any other signal telling them, 'All right, brother or sister, the time is *now*! Let's escape to the North!' And they're out there at night, running and hiding in the caves and the thickets, and rowing for their lives in little skiffs with cruel men and dogs on the banks seeking big rewards for catching them and dragging them back in irons to be tortured until they scream, until they drop! Have *mercy* on them, oh God, and support our work!" The speaker gasped for more breath, and he found it to use in a last appeal, "Let us *all* follow the North Star to the freedom of our souls, which can not be free so long as our brethren are in chains!"

Fletcher wanted to shout out to the

crowd that to his knowledge no such cruelties had ever been inflicted on those black slaves on his family's plantation. He stood feeling as if he'd just been scalded. He wanted to scream to them that his father, his mother, and he himself treated their treasured house slaves practically as members of their family. The slaves knew their place; that was the main difference. He could not truly say what happened to some of the field slaves at the hands of the overseers, because in fact he had heard of some beatings given to discipline a wayward slave or to punish captured runaways. In fact, the only time he'd ever known his mother to scream at his father was the day an overseer who had just caught a runaway came proudly to their mansion's back porch with blood on his coat. "Get that creature away from this house!" his mother had screamed.

The revival shouter called another recently escaped slave to the stage. He silently removed his shirt and turned to reveal his back, whose granulation ridges bespoke a history of many beatings; it resembled a washboard.

The Ellis father and sons had been observing Fletcher's face. No one spoke as the father began leading them back toward the carriage.

Fletcher felt that as a Southerner who had trusted quiet, peaceful-acting Quakers, he had been exploited. Back at the Quakers' home, forcing himself to be civil, he managed to get through most of the dinner before politely excusing himself, hastening to his room, and vomiting up whatever he had eaten.

Back at Princeton, Fletcher was deeply upset. He avoided the Ellis brothers, but at the college library, he reads about the Underground Railroad and the vigilance committees that helped slaves escape.

Reading About the Underground Railroad

He read bent over the materials on his library desk, so that anyone passing close to him would not be likely to identify the subject matter. He'd had no idea that the Underground Railroad had acquired its name around 1831 when an escaping Kentucky slave named Tice Davids jumped into the Ohio River barely ahead of his master and hired slave catchers, who grabbed a boat and rowed their hardest after him, watching him steadily as he swam. He thrashed ashore on the Ohio side, and suddenly dashed from the sight of his baffled and angrily cussing Kentucky pursuers, who could find no trace of him. One exclaimed, "He must've gone off an underground road!" As the story got told over and over, when steam trains were exciting the North, the quote became "underground railroad," and those who helped slave fugitives came to be called "conductors," and "stationmasters," or "brakemen," or "firemen."

As the Northern states made slavery illegal, more and more Southern slaves began trying to escape into the North in search of freedom.

The gradually expanding and improving escape network saw the runaways generally move in the dark of night, frequently led by the Quakers. They and other friends of the fugitives would hide them during the day, and at night escort them to the next safe road or trail or stream. It was a dangerous business, with the fugitives advertised and described in the newspapers, and steadily sought by slave-catchers with their bloodhounds and search warrants and guns. The Underground Railroad agents had to take the boldest of chances, and they risked and sometimes actually lost their own lives when it was they who got captured. And, Fletcher read, of all Underground Railroad activity, the greatest was in Philadelphia.

Finally, in 1850, the Fugitive Slave Law was passed, fining or imprisoning whoever was convicted of helping a slave escape. The Underground Railroad responded with even greater activity than before, with the Quakers in the forefront. Some former slaves risked their lives repeatedly, returning to rescue their families and others left behind. The Maryland black escapee Harriet Tubman returned so often, bringing out so many fugitives, that infuriated white slaveholders pooled an eventual forty thousand dollars as a reward for her capture.

But without white people the Underground Railroad, or UGRR, could not have worked. Fletcher read that some agents went South in their professional capacities as teachers or ministers, for example, using their positions to assist the anti-slavery cause. Others collected information about plantations, their owners, the numbers of slaves and overseers, to feed to the UGRR for its files. Some of these white people were caught, imprisoned, flogged, hanged, or even tortured to death.

Each night after leaving the library, Fletcher would take the longest route back to his dormitory, walking slowly, his mind wrestling with the fact that he had never before known so much about black slaves—or cared to know.

In the following weeks, Fletcher changed his attitude about slavery. He decides to go to Philadelphia again.

In the Offices of the Philadelphia Vigilance Committee

Mr. McDonald, the head of the Philadelphia Vigilance Committee, is meeting with Mr. Marlon, a leader in the Underground Railroad.

On a rainy September morning, the director of the Philadelphia Vigilance Committee, Northern Area, was in the midst of one of his periodic visits with the chief conductor of the Northern Area Underground Railroad.

Their conversation was interrupted when a black former slave, training to become a clerk, knocked at the director's door and, given permission to enter, announced that standing and waiting in the drizzling rain outside was a young white man who said he was from a college and who insisted that he must see the director.

The Vigilance Committee director exchanged a puzzled look with the Underground Railway chief conductor, who said, "I'm just as curious as you are."

"All right, bring him in," the Vigilance Committee director told the clerk.

For a few seconds, the two older men appraised the younger one. It was apparent that Fletcher had not expected to see anyone except Mr. McDonald, the Vigilance Committee director. He was plainly disconcerted.

The director gestured Fletcher to a chair. "We are impressed by your standing out there in the rain, but you have interrupted our meeting, so please be brief."

"I want to volunteer, sir."

"Well, now! So you're a young slaveholder who's going to help us out!"

"Try to trust me, sir."

Even Fletcher realized how ridiculous he sounded. "At least, just hear me, sir—"

McDonald glanced at his clock. "You have five minutes." The director shifted his position within his chair and glanced at his colleague, who nodded.

Fletcher told of his friendship with the Quaker brothers. He described how the antislavery meeting and his reading about slavery had made him want to help the Underground Railroad.

"Now I feel an aversion to slaveholding which has left me with no alternative to coming here to see you today." Hesitating, Fletcher clearly was emotionally drained. "I come to volunteer, sirs, to help in any way I can. So permit me to ask, what can I do to earn your trust?"

McDonald pressed a button. The black

clerk appeared in the doorway. "Bring our North Carolina book."

"Yassuh, right quick."

The two older men did not look at each other; each remained deep within his own thoughts. The clerk returned and set the book on the director's desk.

Thumbing through the book, McDonald found a page, read for a moment, then glanced up at Fletcher.

"Your father's surname also is Randall, and your mother's first name is Ethel, is that correct?"

Fletcher's face was a study in astonished disbelief.

The director began calling names: "Ham, Lem, Caesar, Pompey, Rastus, Chloe, Liza, Luther—do you recognize any of those?"

"No, sir." Fletcher was puzzled.

"So you wish us to believe you're willing to risk your life to help black slaves, when you don't even recognize the names of your own slaves on the plantation you will inherit?"

Fletcher flushed at the barb, but he recovered. "You can't know the names of most of those you help either, can you?"

The director looked at the UGRR chief conductor, nodding at the door, and they both rose as McDonald said to Fletcher, "Will you excuse us for a moment?"

"Of course, sir."

Outside in the hallway, McDonald spoke in a low voice. "What do you really think?"

"Honestly, I am impressed. He's telling the truth, I do believe. It's my first experience with such a young volunteer, but he's smart. He sounds to me capable."

The director said, "In there I was thinking that this young Southerner's background gives him the perfect disguise to be one of your agents."

"We were thinking exactly alike. But I'd want some more time just to mull this over—perhaps to test him somehow."

"Of course. There's no need to rush anything," McDonald reflected.

The two men, McDonald and Marlon, told Fletcher more about the Underground Railroad. They said they would contact him if and when they could use him.

A month later, Fletcher got his orders.

He was told that he was to help a group of 12 slaves escape from his own home area of Ashe County, North Carolina. Six of them would be from his father's plantation!

Fletcher was to make sure that the slaves could travel safely at night through the thick forest and arrive before daybreak at the home of a Quaker "stationmaster" of the Underground Railroad.

Fletcher was to be helped by a local "conductor" who would work with him. McDonald and Marlon did not tell Fletcher his name, but said he would find out who he was by a special signal. The conductor would reveal himself to Fletcher by saying, "Am I your brother?"

When Fletcher arrived home for the Christmas holidays, he acted as if nothing had changed for him. He suggested that his family have a big holiday barbecue on Christmas Eve for all the neighbors. He didn't tell his family his secret reason for the barbecue: It would be a good time for the slaves who were to escape to steal away from their masters.

Fletcher's father loved the idea of the

barbecue. He told Fletcher to hire a neighbor's slave named Harpin' John to organize the barbecue. Besides being an excellent cook, Harpin' John was also a fine harmonica player.

But Fletcher still had not been contacted by the local conductor who would work with him and give the slaves the signal to escape.

"Am I Your Brother?"

Fletcher "borrowed" Harpin' John from his master, Tom Graves, to drive his carriage, called a "landau."

Harpin' John had driven Fletcher and Melissa Anne Aaron, the spoiled daughter of a nearby plantation owner, home from a dance. Fletcher said good night to Melissa Anne, and Harpin' John got the horses ready for the drive home.

Harpin' John had gone to the mansion's backyard well and drawn a wooden bucket of water which he had hurried back for the horses to have a needed drink. The horses finished the water and

Harpin' John reached down and got the bucket as Fletcher walked back toward the landau.

Fletcher said, "Your master, Tom Graves, told me he's instructed you to meet me and my father at our home about twelve o'clock tomorrow, to talk about organizing the barbecue. That means noon-time, and I want you to be sure and be there."

Harpin' John quickly glanced at the still Big House of the Aaron family. Then he turned back and looked piercingly into Fletcher Randall's eyes. "Am I your brother?" he asked.

Fletcher Randall was staggered. He had to steady himself by grasping the top of the tall rear wheel of the carriage. He responded weakly, "I—I am your brother."

Grasping Fletcher's arm, Harpin' John physically helped him on up into the carriage.

Dazed, Fletcher sat back on the carriage's rear double seat as Harpin' John slapped the reins against the horses' rumps and the canopied carriage jerked into motion.

With less than two weeks remaining,

how on earth were they supposed to organize and bring off a mass escape of "a
maximum twelve" to follow the North
Star to safety and freedom!

As if reading Harpin' John's mind,
Fletcher continued, "I thought it might be
best to split the escape into two separate
parties, leaving at different times," he said
tensely.

Harpin' John studied his hands holding
the horse's reins. "Well, since it look like
we good as axin' to die, you got to start
somewhere some listenin' to me—" And
Harpin' John explained that one en masse
escape might be slightly less hazardous.

Fletcher agreed that a single group
could take full advantage of the element
of surprise. Harpin' John added that
among the potential escapees he had in
mind there was only one who had some
leadership experience, "a man what know
the country around in these parts real
good. Like the trail we gonna put this
group on, well, this here man been ten or
more years working in the woods to pick
the best trees to make shingles out of, until
he know that trail right down to the last
coon track. So we can pretty much count

on it that he'll lead 'em straight to that Quaker depot where they supposed to go."

Fletcher said, "I must be honest—I'm still trying to adjust, because quite frankly I'd expected someone white."

"Well, I sho' ain't. An' speakin' truth, I wouldn't of never picked you, neither. But now we stuck with one 'nother, we worry 'bout colors later. But right now we got to trust one 'nother."

Then Harpin' John cupped his harmonica to his mouth, playing a rollicking tune.

"I never knew anyone could make that kind of music on a harmonica," Fletcher said, settling back.

"Me neither when I got hold of one when I was six, an' I been playin' ever since." He looked at the small instrument. "This one my best tools in what you and me doin'."

"How do you mean?"

Harpin' John put the harmonica to his mouth again, and brought forth a vivid sound unmistakably suggesting the chuffing of a railroad locomotive gaining speed. Fletcher leaned forward astonished.

" 'Git on board, li'l chilluns,' that what

that mean—somebody waitin' to escape,"
said Harpin' John. Then he switched to the
soft strains of a black spiritual. "You
know that song's name?" asked Harpin'
John.

"Seems I've heard it, but I can't name
it."

Harpin' John sang, " 'Steal away . . .
Steal away to Jesus—' See? It's a old black
folks' church hymn, that's all white folks
knows if they hear it. But for black folks
ready to escape, it mean now it's time to
go. See, one day if I go ridin' 'round cuttin'
the fool for folks to see, but bein' at the
right times and places, just playin' a little
bit of 'Steal Away,' then nobody couldn't
never say I'd spoke a word, 'cause I
hadn't. But my message got said." He
turned about, looked at Fletcher. "You see
how I mean?"

Abruptly dropping the harmonica back
into his pocket, Harpin' John next cupped
both hands up over his mouth and as his
cheeks puffed, Fletcher smiled, recogniz-
ing the mournful sound.

"Hoot owl," Harpin' John confirmed.
"Now that's my signal if ever one of us gits
lost." He thought a moment. "Got to teach

you to do the hoot owl, too, first chance we git. An' show you some places if we ever need to hide—'cause that could happen!"

Just before they reached the Randall mansion Harpin' John said, "I be here at twelve o'clock tomorrow, to start 'ranging that barbecue. Quick as you can, you got to git you and me clear of your daddy. 'Cause you and me sho' got a whole lot more talkin' to do."

The Escape

December 18, 1855, one week before Christmas, the teenaged son of a plantation overseer was out hunting with his father's best dog. At noontime the boy returned home for lunch. The boy was recounting to his father how he'd failed to find anything to shoot, and he laughingly mentioned that once when he thought the dog had actually treed something, upon investigation it turned out to be nothing but a pile of old quilts and blankets concealed under a heap of dry brush in the bend of a small ravine.

The overseer stopped eating as his son

talked. He waited until the boy finished before saying, "All right, let's go, take me straight to that spot."

By sundown the news was all over Ashe County that a boy hunter with a dog had stumbled upon a fresh pile of quilts and blankets concealed near a trail head. Obviously they were meant for slaves ready to escape, who would need quilts and blankets as they made their way to the even colder North. So by the purest chance, a major escape had been foiled.

As the news spread during the next day, all hell broke loose on the plantations of Ashe and the adjoining counties. Obviously, the escape would not have been haphazard; it had been very carefully planned.

The next afternoon twenty-eight enraged planters, carrying rifles, rode in from both Ashe and the adjoining counties to gather on the veranda of Senator Randall's mansion.

The senator himself was livid. He had insisted that Fletcher be present to experience the problems of planters directly. In a brief, angry session, the planters vowed death to anyone discovered to be involved.

The planters hired more men to patrol to catch the escaping slaves. Fletcher and Harpin' John continue to plan for the escape on Christmas Eve.

The two unlikely UGRR agents calculated that their best camouflage, the one least likely to arouse suspicions, continued to be traveling where they could talk safely in the carriage along the open main road.

But now, even they had to pass the scrutiny of hard-eyed patrollers carrying deer rifles who seemed everywhere, and were often as not augmented by volunteering angry small planters.

"How are we going to get them away in this kind of atmosphere?" Fletcher asked. "It's absolutely deadly! We've got no choice I can see but to delay long enough to let things cool off a bit."

"That ain't likely to be for a good long while," said Harpin' John. "I think we might can do it this comin' Christmas Eve night, like we been plannin'." He looked back and forth in all directions. "I been talkin' to some friends."

"Friends! You mean Quakers?"

"Naw, Quakers some the best friends we got, all right enough. But I been talkin' to some the local Indians."

Harpin' John said, "Right this minute, it's two of them Indian friends hacking through thicket down the back side of the plantation. They hack a covered sort of trail that lead to the New River." He looked at Fletcher. "You know how the New River runs?"

"Northeast, the best I remember."

"You 'members right. One our Indian friends has 'greed to lead our party, in some of their canoes, and he'll get 'em safe and sound to the Quaker depot. That sound all right to you?"

Fletcher grinned. "It sounds just like our orders!" He had to marvel at Harpin' John's ingenuity. And at the astuteness of chief conductor Marlon and the Vigilance Committee's director, McDonald, in having chosen him.

"Oh, yeah, one more thing," Harpin' John continued. "The Indians say they ru-ther leave early in the night. That'll mean our folks will get off during the church pageant instead of like we planned later, during the barbecue party."

Fletcher looked concerned.

"Don't worry, 'cause Indians know what they doin'."

On the day of the planned escape, Christmas Eve, Melissa Anne Aaron has insisted that Harpin' John play his harmonica at the church nativity pageant— the very afternoon of the barbecue and the escape. There is nothing that Harpin' John can do, although his absence can put the slaves' escape in danger.

The nativity pageant had been in progress for almost an hour. A mile and a half away, Fletcher Randall and the planter Tom Graves were patrolling a beat around the Randall mansion veranda, smelling the combined aromas of the pots and tubfuls of the barbecued pork, beef, veal, and chicken.

Fletcher had convinced his mother and father that he should not attend the nativity pageant in order to remain at the mansion in case some guests also might have missed the pageant and would arrive for the Christmas Eve barbecue early. And Tom Graves had joined Fletcher just to ensure that all was going well until his valued slave Harpin' John would be able to return from playing his harmonica for Melissa Anne Aaron at the church pageant.

Two horsemen came pounding up out of the night toward the mansion, and they headed directly for the clustering of lights about the veranda. The lean, slit-eyed chief patrolman Ned Smithers swung down off his horse and came striding directly to meet the advancing Fletcher.

"Bad news, Mr. Randall. It's not what you want to hear on Christmas Eve, but there appears to be a mass escape of slaves in the making. Three are reported missing from the Aaron plantation, and it seems that six are gone from your cabins—a patrolman's checking the premises now, and trying to find out from the rest of the darkies what happened."

Fletcher could imagine the means used to extract the information. He asked, "Are you absolutely certain about this?" He hoped his dismay appeared genuine.

"About as sure as I can be, yessir. I hate to make a mess out of the senator's and your big barbecue affair here, and all—" Fletcher thought that he detected a trace of sarcasm. "But the whole thing seems to have been planned to a fare-thee-well. No telling how long they've been gone." Chief patrolman Smithers paused. "And one more thing, we're looking for Mr. Tom Graves. His wife said we'd probably find him here."

Fletcher heard Tom Graves call from behind him, "Here I am. What's the problem?"

Chief patrolman Smithers turned and nodded to his assistant, who had been standing beside his horse and now came forward, holding a bundle at his side.

Smith took the bundle, which turned out to be a brown suitcoat. He held it up to Tom Graves. "Sir, can you identify this coat?"

"Of course I can," said Tom Graves. "You see my name inked inside the collar. About a year ago I gave it to my slave, the one called Harpin' John."

Fletcher felt a sinking sensation inside his stomach.

"Where is he right now?" Smithers's tone had grown harder.

"You're asking about my slave, my property," said Tom Graves, "so I'm asking why do you want to know?"

"Well, I'll tell you. This coat was found by the patrolman who discovered the slaves were missing. It'd been left behind in one of their cabins. Question is, what was it doing there?"

"Just because you came across that damned coat doesn't mean Harpin' John had anything to do with the escape." Tom Graves was appalled at the prospect of losing a very valuable piece of property, and in truth he would also miss someone as useful and amusing as Harpin' John.

"Maybe not," Smithers said. "But I have to get hold of your slave man and ask him some hard questions, and I think we'll get some truth out of him before we finish. Where can we find him?"

"He's at the church nativity pageant," Fletcher thrust himself into the conversation. "I'll accompany you there. I think it would be best if I went in and brought him out. No need to cause a commotion in church. There'll be the devil to pay soon enough tonight. Once Harpin' John is in your hands, I'll go back and break the news to my father and all the rest."

The four men rode like the wind, and when they arrived at the church Fletcher dismounted first. "I'll be out as quickly as I can," he said, and went inside.

When Fletcher Randall suddenly appeared in the church doorway, the reaction of Parson Brown and his companion Wise Men and Melissa Anne caused the audience to turn their heads. As Fletcher made his way briskly up the church aisle toward the stage, people stared incredulously. Fletcher passed by the front pews, in one of which sat Senator and Mrs. Randall. Their faces were disbelieving as their son stepped up onto the slightly raised stage, past Melissa Anne at her harpsichord, and went straight to black Harpin' John, who stood staring back at him, the harmonica still at his mouth.

"Follow me, *now*!" Fletcher said tautly, and turning abruptly he went double-timing to the door of the pastor's study at the church's right rear, with Harpin' John one step behind him. Once inside the small room, Fletcher asked quickly, "Your horse out back?"

"Yeah, what's happened?"

"No time to talk—" He snatched open the door to the steps outside. They could hear the first rumblings of the church audience. Fletcher barked, "Get your horse, I'll grab somebody else's."

Harpin' John grunted assent, asking no questions. People were starting to emerge from the church and he could hear chief patrolman Smithers shouting as the two horses pounded away into the darkness.

"Let's split up! Go to the place I showed you, I be there!" Harpin' John shouted to Fletcher, pulling his horse toward the right and lying low against its neck to avoid the dangerous low limbs of trees he raced past.

Within the forest, Fletcher's horse stepped into a groundhog's hole, and Fletcher tumbled off as the horse pitched forward, breaking its foreleg and screaming in pain. Fletcher struggled to his feet and then fell onto one knee. His ankle was badly hurt . . . he had never felt more alone.

But then, his chest heaving, he heard the distant hoot-owl sound.

Fletcher put his hands up to his mouth, and tried his best to do what he had been taught.

The hoot-owl call in response was closer.

Harpin' John checked Fletcher's ankle. "Well, we lucky, it ain't broke. But the way it already swellin', look like a real bad sprain." He looked directly into Fletcher's face. "Wasn't sure I'd ever see you no more."

Fletcher said, "I thought you were a goner, too—"

"Would of been, hadn't been for you." Harpin' John took a long pause. "You didn't have to do what you done. How come you come in after me?"

Fletcher thought about that. "Tell you the truth, I never thought about it. I just did, that's all."

"Well, we can't rest here no longer, we got to git movin'. I know they after us, probably with dogs by now, an' we got to be either long gone or hid mighty good by daylight." Again he appraised Fletcher.

"You a big man, but I can carry you to the horse, and us can both ride to a better hiding place."

Fletcher pushed himself upright again, fending away Harpin' John's help, to test himself. He tried the ankle. He winced with the pain. He managed about three hopping steps and stopped.

"It hurts. But I can make steps, especially if I lean on your shoulder. But I'd best wait just a minute—it really hurts."

"Did they all get away?" Harpin' John asked.

"I think. It sounded like it, what little I heard."

"Well, can you tell me what happened, I mean what went wrong?"

"I sure can. You gave somebody a coat, and he left it hanging in his cabin. The patrollers found it with Tom Graves's name inside, and he told them he gave it to you."

"I be damn! You mean 'ceptin' for that, we wouldn't be out here now? All we did, and that one little thing went wrong! If I could've got out'n that pageant, I really b'lieve I'd of noticed old Uncle Ben didn't wear my coat. I should've kept it when he told me he thought it was too pretty for him to wear, anyway."

Harpin' John looked at Fletcher Randall. "Well, for sure, neither one of us can't never go back. What you goin' to do? You figured out yet where you goin'?"

"I haven't had time for that. I wasn't planning on this."

Harpin' John reflected a moment. "You know, lotsa people don't realize how many white folks risks all you got, even your lives, because you don't believe slavery's right."

Fletcher thought a little while. Then he asked, "What about you? Where are you going?"

"Jes' up North, that's all I know for now." Harpin' John chuckled. "Maybe I can start me a little business cookin' good barbecue—I can do that, an' make a little music."

Fletcher determinedly pushed himself up again. He gestured that he was ready to try walking, with Harpin' John's assistance. Two hours later, deeper in the forest, they crossed a wide stream, and were confident they had eluded their pursuers.

Suddenly Harpin' John plucked from his

pocket his harmonica, which he cupped against his mouth, and brought forth his patented resounding railroad locomotive *chuffing* sound.

Abruptly he stopped, whacking the harmonica against one knee. "Hey, lemme quit actin' a fool, 'cause you know what?" He stared up at the radiant North Star, joined by Fletcher. "'Cause this here is Christmas morning now—won't be but a couple of hours 'fore the day breaks."

Again he raised the harmonica, saying to Fletcher, "Now here's a tune I don't know what it is, I jes' sort of remember it from hearin' it last Christmas."

Harpin' John cupped his harmonica. "But I know the tune they played went like this."

He played. Fletcher heard the melody of "Silent Night" as the Christmas moonlight bathed the faces of the black man playing and the white man listening.

When Harpin' John finished, neither man said a word. Then the pair of them resumed walking, silhouetted against the Christmas early morning sky.

Fletcher realized that now his life had changed forever, too. He thought about his parents with a sense of pain and loss that he knew both they and he would be a long time absorbing and coming to terms with. He had made an irrevocable break with his past. He knew he had made a wreck of their lives. His father's political career would become a shambles, and in Senator Randall's eyes, indeed all Southerners' eyes, Fletcher Randall would forever be a traitor. As for his mother, she'd be devastated, and he wondered agonizingly whether she would ever recover from the shame he'd brought upon her, and from the ache of losing her only child. It would be, to both of them, as if he were dead. But whatever the ache of the present and uncertainties of his future, he knew now that by not living for himself, he was learning to live with himself, at last. He'd told Harpin' John that he wasn't sure where he'd go, or what he'd do. But he remembered one thing for sure: he had some friends in Philadelphia.

QUESTIONS FOR THE READER

Thinking About the Story

1. What was interesting for you about the selections from *A Different Kind of Christmas*?

2. Were there ways the events or people in the selections became important or special to you? Write about or discuss these.

3. What do you think were the most important things Alex Haley wanted to say in the selections?

4. In what ways did the selections answer the questions you had before you began reading or listening?

5. Were any parts of the selections difficult to understand? If so, you may want to read or listen to them again. Discuss with your learning partners possible reasons why they were difficult.

Thinking About the Writing

1. How did Alex Haley help you see, hear and feel what happened in the selections? Find the word, phrases or sentences that did this best.

2. *A Different Kind of Christmas* is based on historical facts about the ways slaves escaped using the Underground Railroad. But Alex Haley has also used his imagination to create his own dramatic story. He uses the word "faction" to describe this combination of fact and fiction. What do you think about this technique?

Do you think Haley is "cheating" by using historical facts? Do you think that the historical parts are "spoiled" by becoming part of a made-up story? Is the story more real because the history is true?

3. Writers think carefully about their stories' settings, characters and events. In writing these selections, which of these things do you think Alex Haley felt was most important? Find the parts of the story that support your opinion.

4. In the selections, Alex Haley uses dia-

logue. Dialogue can make a story stronger and more alive. Besides telling the reader what the characters said, the dialogue helps to bring out the personalities of the characters. Pick out some dialogue that made an impression on you, and explain how it helps tell the story.

5. The selection from *A Different Kind of Christmas* is written from the point of view of someone outside the story who tells us what happened. The writer uses the words "he" and "she" as opposed to "I" or "me." What difference does this create in the writing of the selection?

6. Alex Haley, through his writing, makes us understand how a person like Fletcher changes his mind enough about slavery to do something that goes against everything he was raised to believe. Find some parts in the selections that helped you understand how Fletcher arrived at his decision.

Activities

1. Were there any words that were difficult for you in the selections from *A Different Kind of Christmas*? Go back to these words and try to figure out their meanings. Discuss what you think each word means, and why you made that guess. Look them up in a dictionary and see if your definitions are the same or different.

Discuss with your learning partners how you are going to remember each word. Some ways to remember words are to put them on file cards, write them in a journal, or create a personal dictionary. Be sure to use the words in your writing in a way that will help you to remember their meaning.

2. Talking with other people about what you have read can increase your understanding. Discussion can help you organize your thoughts, get new ideas and rethink your original ideas. Discuss your thoughts about the selections with someone else who has read them. Find out if you helped yourself understand the selections in the same or different ways. Find

out if your opinions about the selections are the same or different. See if your thoughts change as a result of this discussion.

3. After you finish reading or listening, you might want to write down your thoughts about the book. You could write your reflections on the book in a journal, or you could write about topics the book has brought up that you want to explore further. You could write a book review or a letter to a friend you think might be interested in the book.

4. Did reading the selections give you any ideas for your own writing? You might want to write about:

- a time you changed your mind about something important.

- a time you went against your family's wishes.

- an event set in a period of history that interests you.

5. Sometimes organizing information in a visual way can help you better under-

stand or remember it. Look at the chronology of events on page 58. You might want to make a similar chronology for a period of history or your family's history.

6. You might interview several people about a recent historical event. Make a list of questions to ask. Afterward, discuss what you learn from these oral histories.

7. If you could talk to Alex Haley, what questions would you ask about his writing? You might want to write the questions in a journal.

ABOUT ALEX HALEY

Alex Haley was born in Ithaca, New York, on August 11, 1921. As a child, he lived with his grandparents in Henning, Tennessee.

Alex Haley is famous as the author of the bestselling novel *Roots*. In *Roots* he traces his family's African origins back to a young man, Kunta Kinte. Kunta Kinte was taken from West Africa around 1765 to become a slave in America. A TV mini-series was made from the book in 1977. It was seen by 130 million Americans.

Before writing *Roots*, Alex Haley served for 20 years in the United States Coast Guard. He taught himself to be a writer during the long sea voyages. After he retired from the Coast Guard, Haley spent several years as a struggling writer in New York City. He became well known when he helped Malcolm X compose his famous *Autobiography*.

Haley spent 12 years doing research for *Roots*. He started with just a few facts that he had heard from his grandmother. His research took him to Africa, where he learned about the lives of the people who were brought to this country as slaves.

As he did in *Roots*, Alex Haley bases *A Different Kind of Christmas* on facts and some real people, but he uses his imagination to create other characters and a dramatic story. Haley uses the word "faction" to describe this combination of historical fact and fiction.

A CHRONOLOGY OF EVENTS
RELATED TO SLAVERY

1619   The first slaves are brought to North America. Slavery is practiced throughout the country, North and South.

1688   Quakers in Philadelphia protest "the traffic in the bodies of men."

1774   Rhode Island, a northern state, is the first to outlaw slavery.

1793   The cotton gin is invented, making growing cotton more profitable and slaves more valuable.

1793   The first Fugitive Slave Law is enacted. This law made it illegal to prevent the arrest of runaway slaves.

1804   New Jersey is the last northern state to outlaw slavery.

1807   Congress prohibits importing slaves from Africa.

1830   The term "Underground Railroad" begins to be used to describe secret escape routes for runaway slaves.

1838   Philadelphia's Vigilance Committee is founded by Robert Purvis.

1850   The second Fugitive Slave Law is enacted.

1855   The time Alex Haley's *A Different Kind of Christmas* takes place.

1860   Abraham Lincoln is elected president.

1861   The American Civil War begins. Eleven southern states leave the Union. One of the most important issues of the war was whether slavery should be allowed at all in the United States.

1863   The Emancipation Proclamation frees all slaves in the southern states.

1865   The Civil War ends.

1865   The Thirteenth Amendment, abolishing slavery, becomes part of the United States Constitution.

ABOUT THE
UNDERGROUND RAILROAD

When people are forced into slavery, they often attempt to escape. This was especially true of black slaves in the United States. It was not until around 1830, however, that efforts to help runaway, or fugitive, slaves became well organized. People started using the name Underground Railroad (UGRR) to describe the secret escape routes to freedom.

The UGRR was not a real railroad. The escaping slaves did not ride railway cars, nor did they travel under the ground. They went on foot, traveling by night and hiding by day.

In the UGRR system, escaping slaves were called "passengers," "packages" or "freight." The homes or caves that sheltered them were "stations," and the men and women who guided the runaways were "conductors."

Conductors on the UGRR often posed as travelers, peddlers or slave traders. Once they had helped a group of slaves escape, they would guide them along a route through backwoods and swamps and over mountains. Stations were usually about 10 miles apart.

The UGRR had dozens of routes, or "lines," that reached from the slave states across the North and into Canada. Between 40,000 and 100,000 blacks reached freedom via the UGRR. The heaviest activity on the UGRR was in Illinois, Indiana, Ohio and Pennsylvania. There were even escape routes that took escaped blacks west across the Mississippi River.

Vigilance Committees supported the work of the UGRR. Made up of both blacks and whites, the committees were active in many cities. They gave the runaway slaves clothes, food, money and legal help. Philadelphia's Vigilance Committee, founded in 1838 by a free black man named Robert Purvis, was the strongest of all.

Helping slaves escape was a violation of the Fugitive Slave Laws. These laws were passed in 1793 and 1850 and required the return of escaped black slaves. Because of these laws, many runaway slaves went to Canada, where the law did not apply. But many dared to stay in the United States and, with the help of both whites and free blacks, they started new lives in the North.

There was danger in both "riding" and operating the UGRR. A recaptured slave could be cruelly punished, and conductors who were caught faced prison sentences under the Fugitive Slave Laws. Some conductors were tortured and killed.

Free blacks played a large part in the operation of the UGRR. So did slaves on plantations along the way. The UGRR also received help from people who were not part of the UGRR organization. Such citizens might shelter runaway slaves for just a night.

Members of the Quaker religion were important leaders in the UGRR. As early as 1688, Quakers in Philadelphia protested "against the traffic in the bodies of men and the treatment of men as cattle." As time went on, the Quaker sect forbade its members to own slaves.

Many southern Quakers moved to the North because of their hatred of slavery. They established UGRR centers in Ohio, Indiana and Pennsylvania.

A Quaker named Levi Coffin, born in North Carolina, hated the cruelty to slaves that he saw. After he moved to Indiana and later to Ohio in 1847, his home became a major station on the UGRR. Coffin, who helped about 3,000 slaves escape, was sometimes called the president of the UGRR.

Harriet Tubman, known as the Moses of her people, was one of the most daring conductors on the UGRR. After escaping from slavery, she traveled back to the South 19 times, personally helping more than 300 slaves gain their freedom.

The UGRR increased northern sympathy for the slaves, and it angered many Southerners. It was one factor that increased the hostility between North and South before the Civil War.

Seven series of good books for all readers:

WRITERS' VOICES
Selections from the works of America's finest and most popular writers, along with background information, maps, and other supplementary materials. Authors include: Kareem Abdul-Jabbar • Maya Angelou • Bill Cosby • Alex Haley • Stephen King • Loretta Lynn • Larry McMurtry • Amy Tan • Anne Tyler • Abigail Van Buren • Alice Walker • Tom Wolfe, and many others.

NEW WRITERS' VOICES
Anthologies and individual narratives by adult learners. A wide range of topics includes home and family, prison life, and meeting challenges. Many titles contain photographs or illustrations.

OURWORLD
Selections from the works of well-known science writers, along with related articles and illustrations. Authors include David Attenborough and Carl Sagan.

FOR YOUR INFORMATION
Clearly written and illustrated works on important self-help topics. Subjects include: Eating Right • Managing Stress • Getting Fit • About AIDS • Getting Good Health Care, among others.

TIMELESS TALES
Classic myths, legends, folk tales, and other stories from around the world, with special illustrations.

SPORTS
Fact-filled books on baseball, football, basketball, and boxing, with lots of action photos. With read-along tapes narrated by Phil Rizzuto, Frank Gifford, Dick Vitale, and Sean O'Grady.

SULLY GOMEZ MYSTERIES
Fast-paced detective series starring Sully Gomez and the streets of Los Angeles.

WRITE FOR OUR FREE COMPLETE CATALOG:

Signal Hill Publications
P.O. Box 131
Syracuse, NY 13210-0131